Cor Meum Poetry

POETRY OF MY HEART

Richard Patterson

COR MEUM POETRY
POETRY OF MY HEART

iUniverse books may be ordered through booksellers or by contacting:

iUniverse
1663 Liberty Drive
Bloomington, IN 47403
www.iuniverse.com
1-800-Authors (1-800-288-4677)

ISBN: 978-1-5320-8433-1 (sc)
ISBN: 978-1-5320-8432-4 (e)

Library of Congress Control Number: 2019914783

Print information available on the last page.

iUniverse rev. date: 10/18/2019

Contents

Dennis' War

Flanders fields and poppies, it's not,
but Vietnam jungles with its stink and it's rot.
The Great war a stupid war,
the Jungle war the very same score.
Forgetting Augustines justified wars,
the diplomats and generals walk night through that door.
It's the blood of the boys that will water these fields,
the maimed and the dying just where they kneel.
Lets posture and bicker who sits where,
while another unknown son dies on an unnamed hill.
No tree of liberty watered by their precious blood,
this nothing more than a vile crimson flood.
You old men come and have your look,
tour the headstones listed in the tourist books.
Dennis my friend I loved him so well,
died in the Jungle just where he fell.
he could not care less nor pronounce the name,
of that foreign village that staked its death claim.
His and his brothers blood drenched the ground,
we back home never hearing a sound.
Their sacrifice on our soft behalf,
our home town flags flying half-mast.
We must fight our wars if we are attacked,
all other conflicts we should just stand pat.
Our boys blood too precious to spill at unnamed villages and unknown
hills.
I am sure Dennis would rather have been in his mother's arms,
she singing a lullaby until breaking dawn.

1

We should review what Augustine had to say;
War should be limited and proceed in this way.
I want our boys to grow up so strong and not have their bodies littering fields
where they don't belong.
If they must die let them die here,
defending our liberty and our freedoms so dear.

Taking Sunday Off

No church today,
no rules to obey.
These edicts subdue,
I have too much to do.
I will be free,
I am a rebel you see.
I am out and about,
fellow rebels start to shout.
But as I partake of this wonderful steak,
I squeak out a feeble prayer.
Other rebels took note;
he's a fraud a turncoat;
we thought he was a rebel we swear.
A quite voice inside say the rules are a guide,
not to subdue and rule over you.
So, a rebel I ain't,
but just your ordinary Saint.

The Cursed on a Tree

The godlessness of this wretched old cross,
for our fate such a horrendous loss,
for us a death is just what we need,
but crucifixion a bit much indeed!
The king of the Jews hanging limp on a tree;
for you and for me, but for knave or a slave?
No loincloth but naked,
His circumcision revels,
Shame upon shame as we jeer, and we squeal.
This hideous creature let's hate him some more;
Just another bar Jesus, oh what a bore.
Every filthy sin on my part,
Every little crook of my heart;
Plunging the depths of my soul.
I catch my breath with a start,
How we relish this part.
We hated this man, he means nothing to me,
with his teaching and hard sayings,
he's a fraud can't you see.
With my anger and lust, let this show conclude,
I am wasting my time; I've got much work to do.
As the law certainly states,
the cursed hangs from a tree;
there's really not much more here to see.
God's judgement comes down with a thunderous blow,
and crushes this man from his head to his toe.
Oh, by the way, where is God to be found?
In his silence, he stands on this most hollowed ground.

4

But we walk away; already bored of this tiring display.
As we all depart and the sword thrust his heart,
let's put all this nonsense into the grave and the dark.
As I stumble and waiver and go astray,
I hear demons and devils start to cackle and bray.
We are of such a sophisticated mind,
Jew's on Sunday and Greeks most of the time.
Stumbling block and foolishness this old cross;
no way in the world will it burn off this dross.
The disciples knowing this much as they fled;
leaving this poor man to die as he bled.
This blasphemer is deserving of such a godless death;
our evil hearts rejoice as we lay him to rest,
Death triumphs with its filthy stench;
sadistic and cruel it destroys in a pinch.
It appears this God-man absorbed all of this wrath,
as the God of creation made this a holy blood bath.
Into the tomb where this man was laid,
all nerves in heaven and hell were frayed;
who knew how this scene was to play.
But God had a plan beyond all comprehend,
all foolishness and sin will come to an end.
Death and hades will not prevail;
from the grave comes Jesus;
of him we shall hail!
He ascended on high to reside
with the ancient of days,
to all of creations wonder and praise.
He sends the Spirit to comfort and teach;
we are not left as orphans,
by his grace he does preach.

Death oh death you can sting us no more,
Jesus took all sins and all them he bore.
This second gardener bringing life out of death,
as Adam's great sins were all laid to rest.
As I exhale with a cosmic sigh,
this hole in my heart is filled with God's beauteous eye.
A breath of grace blows across my face;
with His help I can finally finish this race.
Oh my God, what shame and sin do I have,
as I tortured and mocked your fair hearted Lad.
I really revile my pitiful self;
I will weep and wail in all my travails.
This king of all kings who reigns from a tree,
with his wooden cross, he battles for you and for me.
My God, my God, my posture should be,
my hand on my mouth and my face to my knees.
Thank you Lord Jesus the rest of my days,
as you say to me come and just stay.
Jesus my lord I must repay and serve,
but you say stop and just eat;
all of eternity I will serve you at this holy feast.
This is a gift that you cannot repay;
so, recline at my table by my side as you lay.

Losing Our Minds

Saying goodbye and a long farewell,
to a friend or a brother
fills my heart with trouble.
Memory shadows start to lengthen,
as inner resolve tries to strengthen.
This internal battle with its inevitable end,
the person disappears and emptiness wins.
There are moment's when recognition breaks through,
connecting and being for a brief interlude.
These are the times when God gives us a glimpse,
of this loved one's life before it was spent.
In and out of these moments my friend comes and goes,
time will of course cause even these to slow.
It's difficult to watch this slow waltz of doom;
around they go in an ever diminishing room.
Now it's just sitting and looking off into space,
leaving us to wonder what's behind that blank face.
However unknowingly he goes or stray's he's even now
our "sacrifice of praise" the anthem we raise.
Every path he now strolls is covered with flowers,
as Christ now holds him with strong arms of power.
Walking refreshed I now know of this bliss;
I am no longer afraid of this unknowable abyss.
You are leaving us behind as your now is the past;
with the best of God's favor,
you leave us at last.

Losing My Religion

"Losing my religion" a heartfelt song by Daigle,
made me stop and wonder;
is religion a manmade fable?
Man loves to build towers,
and work his way towards heaven,
whether in the high places or baking bread unleavened.
The early church in Acts,
guided by Christ and Spirit,
practiced good religion,
few rules and no division.
In pure religion, this is what you strive for,
helping widows, orphans and the many poor.
It didn't take too very long,
before it's confounded to it's core.
The church in its worldly splendor,
ceased helping widows and the poor.
Church with its magisterium's,
took its eyes off of Christ,
burdening man like Pharasee's,
now we have done it twice.
We must now perform like marionette's dancing at a play,
forgetting Christ's teaching and the reason He was slayed.
I don't want man's religion to confuse me and to rule,
I will go with the Scriptures,
and learn in God's holy school.

Liv

Oh, Liv of life with eyes twinkling bright,
Sweet wandering fancy-
charmed child.
With unkept tresses so tossed and so wild;
What have you spied upon now?
Things overlooked in crannies and nooks,
magic and colors in many a hue,
but to us it's all just old news.
From whence this wonderment I've lost it somehow,
Liv teach me the ways of your soul,
it seems I've lost my way as I became old.
It's this little thing and it's that little thing;
open your eyes and you will see.
Can you hear that sound,
can you taste that brown,
can you hear the purple and green,
there is just so much more to be seen.
Oh, the small voice Liv it is your choice to listen to her indeed;
and as you speed in your world of dreams she is a friend you'll see.
Oh, Liv as fair as a fairy's breath with her laugh and her joy complete;
I have much to learn and unlearn too as the fairy's dance at your feet.
Rest assured and be assured as sure as you can be,
much of Liv that we think we know,
but much a mystery.
As she grows her life unfolds, dancing to her tune.
Don't think you have her figured out she will leave you with a little doubt.
I am glad that Liv is in my life a gift from God it's true.

She sees the sights with such delight the purples and greens and blue.
Many blessings Liv upon your head,
as you grow so very old;
harken back to times long past when this your story was told.

Moonbeam and rainbow

I stood upon the edge of a vast and empty
place and gazed beyond,
the emptiness could be my soul
a vastness with no bounds.
But I can look past the null and
the void and find a rainbow
which sets the standard for that
day. Out of the darkness the moonbeam
lights my way, the lonely sound
is but the cadence of my heart
propelling me past this place and
time; the secret is tomorrow's promise.
We must go and step into the moonbeam's path
and claim a rainbow for ourselves.

The Work of a Master

The Master had a plan so grand,
emptiness of nothing by itself would not stand.
From nothing comes everything
word and its complete,
a most astounding feat.
This sovereign God,
Creator divine;
the God-head knew that it was time.
Out of love for three we will create he,
and he will forever be.
A vice-regent who by the two joined to rule and all subdue;
even this we made just for you.
A world of greens and blues and various hues,
reds and yellows and violet too,
mix them thoroughly through and through
and endless colors descend upon you.
Now he adds something never heard,
sounds upon myriad sounds;
a tinkling here a roar over there;
a chirp a cry and a very soft sigh.
-when these colors are added to these wonderful sounds,
then every glory to you rebounds.
You add the fragrance's,
odors and smells and who of us can ever tell of the wonders of you three,
as you create this for all to see.
You are beyond all pale and every magical tale.
Every creature, flower large or small,
all things are in your rapturous thrall.

Planets and all cosmic things held by intricate design;
the mathematics and movements are ever so sublime.
A little here, more over there it's beyond my feeble mind.
Some things I see I describe with ease,
but explanations I cannot grasp;
all I have is my faith at last.
You are so vast from times long past,
I tremble with a shaking fear;
How could you my mighty God,
to me be ever so near?
I am a wavering reed,
a smoldering wick compared to you my soul is so sick.
But you take pride in all of us,
as you made us from your holy dust.
How could we have run so far from you shaking our fists so high?
Pathetic little worms with pride,
from your eyes we cannot hide.
But I cannot help myself as I sit up my kingdoms to fail;
even I know they will not prevail.
So once more I stop and then I drop and roll out my repeated repents,
as your grace and mercy is once again for me most heaven sent.
Pray tell me Lord what is wrong with me as woe after woe I endlessly see?
I know you made me in your perfect image
but I am a disaster of my parents' linage.
I know what resides inside this temple,
it's just sin and it's really that simple.
I've taken creation and made it my god;
instead of the pot I should give God my nod.
As Paul the apostle stated so eloquently,
I am the chief of sinners and that is entirely me.
I need some help outside of myself;

meditation and philosophies won't do.
Jesus, I need your Father and Spirit and You,
as you heal me through and through.
I want to enjoy the wonder of you,
the music I tenderly hear;
all glory resides in heaven above and also very near.
Who is like you precious Dear who knows all our dreams and fears.
Oh my God you are so great as you nailed my sins on that terrible stake
and defeated that most ancient of snakes.
All praise and glory to King Jesus we hail as he binds up our wounds
and all of our ails.
There is so much more glory for us to see then I can ever say,
but let me try just today,
to ponder this in your azure skies,
as my mind with love doth rise.

Our Republic

Let freedom ring not hollow and stale,
but bright and noisy with much regale.
For each and every denizen but specially for its citizen.
You alien and sojourner,
stay calm as you learn our ways, laws and healing balm.
Don't try to change our tradition, our culture,
resist the temptation to rupture.
Calm your spirits and your nerves,
learning ways that you might serve.
America, man's ingenuity,
Gods laws given intuitively
As per Aquinas and the Scriptures,
many years and then you are a fixture;
of this grand and glorious land,
holding our hands as we now plan.
The wisdom of our founders,
knowing democracy always flounders,
constructed our republic so fine,
history teaching all other forms of government being blind.
The tyranny of the majority unable to checkmate the minority.
Our laws and rights bestowed by the great Divine
not to be thwarted by man's feeble design.
We must be educated,
civil and kind so this republic will prosper and shine.
A city of hope on a shining hill,
let's nurture Lady Liberty and fight for her still!

Daughter Over the Water

Speak softly speak slowly the wind is a-crying;
it appears our sweet daughter lies a-dying.
This is the moment and time for crying.
Her face passes over the waters
oh, where are you going my precious daughter?
Quite now and hear what the wind has said;
it appears our dear daughter is now lying dead.
No more her face over the waters,
we have now lost our most fair daughter.
The funeral dirge is heavy and slow,
we have no time for ribbons or bows.
As the painful music drifts over the water,
it seems as if we never had a daughter.
With the moss and the violets near the resting stone,
it seems to me all of creation moans.
Why did you pass over the cold cold water
my sweet and precious daughter?
I should have held you firmly fast,
And prayed to God that this might pass.

Man Journey

I am born my slate is clean, I am neither mean nor am I serene, and
I rapidly start to grow, like a springbok leaping to and fro.
I have such vigor in my bones, there's really no reason for me to atone.
Rushing headlong to become a man,
many things my father cannot understand.
Must I continue to teach him the truth,
I am wise with knowledge it must be my youth.
This was a sprint with me, myself, and I,
in a quick twenty years, I will eat manhood pie.
Now I have entered this warrior stage.
My God I feel bold and so very brave,
with my band of brothers get out of our way.
Oh, to look upon me at this time,
swashbuckling with pride I might be divine.
But how we need men such as these, nothing's impossible with them on their
steeds.
Battling, protecting the women and poor, these stories belong in all our folklore.
But twenty years of this takes its toll, I do feel bold, but in creeps the old.
Before I know it, the years have gone past, now I am entering my kingdom at last.
As I arrive and survey all my domaine, much lucre, family and all wordly fame,
there is not much more that I can claim,
as I settle down into my frame.
There is nothing much more for me to master; I have succeeded in avoiding life's

greatest disasters.

I go about marking out my spots; a jot, a tittle a check and a dot,

This time as a king it seems so long,

but I look around and my children are gone.

I notice more grey and white coming on,

I catch my breath this must make me strong.

But now the vim and vigor I had, as I danced and pranced a dark headed lad.

So late I see now so sublime, were these

the fast fleeting moments in time.

Now as I start to slowly descend

I become a sage and a wit with a pen.

People come and sit at my feet, I have much to say, its all of my treat.

I am sixty or seventy years of age,

and I find it hard to remain a sage,

there is sin of pride, I have nowhere to hide.

There is really nothing much more to say, if a man arrives here, it's where most

will stay.

But in God's mercy and tenderest love,

some he will give a most gentle shove.

It's back to the place where I first began

I am a lover of presence; this is where I will stand.

This time will be brief and to my relief, instead of just me I am a lover of thee.

It's taken a lifetime for me to see, it's love and love only for you and for me.

Man's Agony

Job of old spoke of the morning stars singing,
As God was creating the cosmos he sent winging.
The angels all nodded with approving assent
as God made man with more of descent.
Fabulous, gorgeous Lucifer smiled,
and he knew he was better than these by a mile.
But God said wait Lucifer and take your hosts,
I have made you all to serve these with a toast.
But Lucifer with pride saw these men as weak;
I will be damned I won't serve them,
they are to me so meek.
God said Lucifer you now must go,
and by the way take your third of angels in tow.
Lucifer was created with a seal of perfection,
the anointed cherubim without dereliction.
Now filled with violence and cast as profane,
there is now no glory in any of his names.
Your heart lifted up by beauty and wisdom;
corrupted by splendor,
love for God rather slender.
Lucifer fell like a lightning bolt,
but this old serpent is no mental dolt.
Brilliant and wise this master devil uses all his disguise:
poor man will take the brunt of this devil's hand,
as we are so far from being wise.
Since we as men are bent to sin,
it is easy for us to invite this angel in.

He started with Adam and Eve who were both deceived with surprising ease;
a word or two out of place and mankind was off to the race.
Those supernatural battles are mostly out of our sight,
as this cosmic contest gives Satan much delight.
Daniel was given just a hint,
when Michael the archangel was delayed in his sprint.
Satan is not one to be trifled one bit;
all the lost people are on his death list.
James says he's like a lion about,
consuming sinners and placing a ring in their snouts.
He entices with lust, power and fame,
as he lies to us that's actually his name.
Oh how we humans are so easily deceived,
this antichrist leads us with the utmost of ease.
We will run from our Father of Lights,
as we chase after Applyon with squeals of delight.
As we dance in the square to Satan's tune,
we are on rotting parchment just out of doom.
The fires of hell belch sulphurious gas,
as we dance and prance in a deadly trance.
We are dangling by the slenderest of threads,
as the flames lick and leap and fill us with dread.
I hear moans and groans and gnashing of teeth;
every sermon and prayer I try to repeat.
I am about to faint, it all seems so queer;
If I call on Jesus, I have nothing to fear.
But now it appears it might be too late;
I have rejected the Savior, and this is my fate.
God is good and gives us good gifts;
witness man a most perfect fit.

So, in hell no light just perpetual night
with continuous bawling as we forever keep falling.
Friends are good but these we repel,
as no good exists in this kind of hell.
No restrainer to retard our increasing evil,
we give feast to sins ravenous weevils,
in agony and anguish this worm never dies;
gnawing and chewing it has its free ride.
This worm was my most favorite sin,
and in the end, I lose, and it wins.
As Lazarus told Abraham of old,
and I am now telling you;
seek after God in all that you do.
Please do not believe the detestable lie,
as I did and now, I just want to die.

Coughing

As I catch my breath with strains of a heaving chest;
a raspy gurgling toil.
The wheezes and rattles on monotonous replay;
what I need now is a brand-new display.
From whence this disease invading my ease,
it just came in and didn't say please.
Now the weak link in this body of mine,
It appears it rests in my lungs I find.
If there is something that will take me out,
it's the impedance of my breath going in and out.
A hacking and whacking and coughing a fright;
this battle rages throughout the night.
The heaving and violence of the coughing I swear,
I check my eyeballs,
are they still there?
This two-note symphony of harks and barks,
gives fair warning this is no mere lark.
Now I have been sick with this one time before,
lying just outside of deaths bad door.
But after seven or ten days I learned,
this time was not going to be my turn.
Right now, I am on a five-day ride;
a few more day's I am on the healthy side.
But I have a sense of what might take me out;
as coughing, hacking and death rattles about.

Lucy Joy

Lucy Joy a girl she was born,
and not a boy it was to our great joy.
She imprinted on us and her stamp was sure,
a lady she would be and quite demure.
Her attire being all dresses,
she eschewed the look of the Hess' es;
knowing what she liked many suggestions she spiked;
sensing what was just right.
She was knit in the tenderest of details,
as God being her master, she cannot fail.
She is bursting with love and it won't be contained,
kisses cascading as a refreshing rain.
This treasure trove a gift from above,
all kisses and hugs an avalanche of love.
I don't believe I've seen one so effusive,
but this best describes our precious Lucy.
Oh God, how she loves most times to laugh,
and rare is the times when she would rather spat.
She loves to color, draw and do girly stuff,
there is little about her that likes playing rough.
Sometimes she sits quietly as if in a trance,
scheme's and dreams in her head they must dance.
Her speech is lilting and somewhat unique,
where are the R's we ask and beseech?
Rapidly she speaks and word becomes wood,
harper is hopper if the R's only could.
It's delightful to hear this sing and this song,
the R's will be found it shouldn't take long.

Nothing eludes her quick little glance,
"how are you feeling, would you like to dance?"
She is alert and sharp as a fine edge knife;
nothing is missed from her view and her sight.
Lucy's heart is tender and so true,
she sympathies with other's their trials and their rue's.
Still, she is so very young,
it's going to be fun to witness her run.
Lucy is given us a sparkling jewel,
God will guide her in His all perfect school.

Jeremiah

This priestly young man charged by God to stand,
soon learned his life would be less than grand.
No marriage, no children few friends to claim,
spoke against Judah it's sin and Lamentable shame.
This weeping prophet reluctant for sure,
preached God's word for Judah's healing cure.
Forty years tortured and sorely tried,
was faithful to God but often he cried.
Baruch a rare friend and steadfast scribe,
was with him in Egypt by his side as he died.
The lesson for me from this man's life,
is God may use us and it might cause us strife.
Jeremiah often wanted to run and escape,
but leaned into God's mercy and wonderful grace.
A man of such immense faith,
he stands out as one of the greats.
The psalms say praise God in all that we do,
the weeping prophet Jeremiah to this he was true.

Love Counts

Oh, God how I love thee,
let me count the way's;
I know it's more than the poets ever can say.
From the end to the start,
countless thoughts fill my heart.
Love is more than agape,
Eros or id,
capturing my heart,
it did what it did.
I will strive with words as love comes into view;
and go with St. Peter declaring,
Lord you know that I do."

Doubt

From sin surcease as you guide my feet,
to salubrious air to your heaven so fair.
Lachrymose no more as I rap on your door,
you call me by name from your far distant shore.
I often fear my ultimate fate,
am I your sheep are you the gate?
Expurgate this awful dread,
I am for sure alive and certainly not dead.
I need the faith of a saint like Daniel,
but mine is a faith more like a scandal.
I want your assurance that I can finish my race with endurance.
I must wait to see is it grace for me;
or must I stand alone before your holy throne.

He's with Me

Lift up your head O ancient gates,
open wide O ancient doors,
there is only one that you adore.
Only one with pure heart righteous and holy may pass through this
door;
mighty in battle and a warrior indeed,
is the Lord of Host's upon his steed.
King of Kings passes on through,
bidding all others, a distant adieu.
I lift my hands in feeble awe,
trying my best to just keep the law,
again, I fail as I fall.
I realize my faith is pathetically weak,
I believe but unbelief is what abounds,
it's a guide I need to show me around.
I ponder Abraham this man of old,
his faith counted righteous which made him like gold.
He has learned much in his one-hundred years,
the next seventy-five obeying the Lord the one he did fear,
ascending Mount Moriah with Isaac a
"sacrifice of praise", God staying his blade before he could slay.
He loved God more than he loved his son,
truly I fail when it's all said and done.
Oh, I can't countenance to see myself as I am;
a talker, a hypocrite, a coward I stand.
Truth be known I don't love God as I should;
it's all posture and positioning,
I would if I could.

I love my sons,
my children my wife,
Friends and things and even my life.
Saul divinated the witch of endor falling from his perch of Kingly
splendor.
Starting strong but ending weak,
committing Seppuku upon his blade so sleek.
His name written in the hall of shame,
never achieving any Davidic fame.
Abel, Enoch, Noah and Moses, Abraham, Isaac and Jacob too,
Joseph, Samuel, Gideon also;
Rahab the harlot all had such faith,
while my heart is scarlet.
God told Abraham to spare his son,
God took his perfect child and through death was undone,
the parallel of these events are not lost upon me,
the death of Jesus a gift unto me.
And as my floundering's and flailing's abound,
I hear my name as many waters resound.
King Jesus I know I am one that he chose,
of many to ascend and pass through the doors and travel
and worship at his distant shore.

My Lament

I confess I know my wicked heart.
The world has riches and I want my part.
Pride in my heart that's where is starts.
I have tried to keep my heart pure
and my feet on this rock firm and sure.
Vindicate the accused and the one whose weak.
Do justice to the one who's meek,
rescue the one who cannot speak.
We are flesh and like wind we pass away.
I have sinned and I know I go astray.
when I pondered this, I was troubled in my heart,
but you sized me by the hand
and you counseled me.
Whom have I in heaven but you?
I desire nothing else
God the strength of my heart and my
portion forevermore;
the nearness of God is good for me.
As you arise O Lord all foundations are shaken;
arise God and judge.

A Car Trip

I made her cry
it wrenched my heart.
The day I remember well,
Why? I think it was
hormones, me confused in
a roil- she vulnerable
and all knowing. But the
gauntlet had been laid
I must move away. Birthing
is lifelong and always
painful. I want to tell
her things- speak to her
at the lowest of levels
a rumbling note, my heart
bursts with the effort but
sons and mothers cannot cross
that chasm; at least not
this time around.

Despair

I have this sense of despair,
nothing seems aright when I am breathing this air;
I just retreat deeper into my lair.
My world has lost its usual glow,
I am travelling now alone in this deeper darker abode.
I arrived here of a sudden it seems,
with no allowances made for my usual dreams.
This sadness takes hold of my poor wretched soul;
dolefully it takes it's slow measured toll.
Why try I cry but then I buy the lie as a part of me just wants to die.
The friends I once knew it seems they just flew away from me;
my heart is in painful anguish.
What did I do?
Was I not a good friend as they melted away and I pleaded just stay.
So, I am down to only a few and at this news I weep, and I rue.
This pushes me deeper still, as I languish in this deadly swill.
What's the point at this time in my life,
I stumble and stare at things not right.
Life beats you down to the very ground,
my joy has lost its musical sound.
This pity I have, I've had it before,
it's all about me and not one person more.
I must find the exit door and escape from this dreadful land of the poor.
I need to focus on other than me and pray to God a light I will see.
These cycles come closer as I age,
and I realize it's just an endless stage.
We fight and rage as we beat back the dark
as I long to walk in God's beautiful park.

32

Lily Marie

Oh, Lily Marie wholesome and fair,
with your long flaxen reddish hair;
how you came upon our scene and blew us all to smithereens.
Prancing buff upon the table,
as a little thing you were able;
to recite the numbers and the letters
at all such things you just seemed better.
The freckles sprinkled upon your face,
It's your smile they seem to embrace.
Your eyes sparkling clean and clear,
hiding all things that you hold dear.
Your laughter and your impeccable wit,
all such things a perfect fit.
God has given you a beautiful mind,
It will serve you well time after time.
People like to be around you,
and as a friend you are very true.
Virtue is your worth and creed,
while riding scriptures on your steed.
A young woman with so much hope,
all possibilities fill your boat.
It's fun to be around you too,
as we play a game or two.
It seems that you always win,
amidst the laughter and clattering din.
Your brothers and your sisters
dear are so blessed to have you near.
To our bosom we will take,

of this girl of whom we spake.
My Lily where are you going so fast,
it always seems we are following last.
It appears you have so much to do,
know I lay down my heart for you.
My first grandchild it seems to me,
closes the circle without any seams.
Beautiful, whimsical, and lovely yes,
some of the adjectives that describes her best.
Ireland with its greens and golds,
coursing through her with the ancients of old.
Sweet Lily please come and sit,
and I will converse a bit with a wit.

Music

The music is soft and haunting, the
words drift to me and comfort me
like an old friend. Melodies with a
certain warmth and sensuousness. The
cold rain falls, and the music covers
me and keeps me warm,
my inner peace is again nurtured.

Floating Free

When I think upon this thought,
all other thoughts come to naught.
Who am I to think upon me,
a speck of dust just floating free.
An atom in space, and in time,
the cosmos swallows all,
neither harsh nor kind.
A worm floating free in endless space;
an icy cold worm just tumbling in place.
But I am different from all other things,
I reason and think this gift given to me;
the cosmos and all shudders at this worm you see.
If I am a worm a glow worm I shall be.
At this I should pause and give praise to my maker;
but we all know what resides in this temple, a sin shaker.
I am smug in my assessment of the Imago Dei,
no other thing was made in this way.
In my sin warped view, I am perfect it's true;
forgetting I am imperfect,
an image for sure.
Sitting in a room all alone,
no stimulus no prodding only my thoughts forlorn.
These thoughts are maddening and frightening to me,
my time better spent praying to Thee.
I must be distracted give me a trifle or two;
silence and nothingness my mind won't go around these,
give me distraction,
joy and even calamities;

I understand these.
Paschal in his Pensee's wrote of life's myriad ways;
we should all slow down and read what this sage had to say.
We are only men made by God's nod.
Judging angles, we are judged by him,
Maker of all even the wind.
Thank God for Jesus in my puffery and pride,
as He slew sin and made it to die.
It's true I am a thinker but not The Thinker;
I am a counterfeit,
a vapor not a seminal maker.
Imperfectly reiterating what He has revealed;
I know nothing,
at this point I should just kneel.
What presumption on my part as I presume on His heart.
My theology distilled down to this point;
pot and Potter nothing speaks louder.
And as I float through this empty space,
one thing I know my name will not be erased.

A Nations Shame

Seven black clad jurists non constitutional for certain,
rendered a verdict a curse demons dancing behind curtains.
Motherhood, fatherhood, childhood
blew cold as a nation quietly gave up its soul.
Little Jack, little Jill would not climb up their hill,
no chance for greatness nor even a spill.
Knitted and weaved ensconced in their womb,
never imagining this would be their tomb.
Mother for us is standing her ground,
no cause to worry about that sucking sound.
My sister Jill terror upon her face,
in a moment she's gone without even a trace.
My mother, my protector, my darling dear,
my limbs they are gone,
then my heart now departs.
Oh, how we debate the fine points of death,
as we obey at Molech's satanic behest.
Gosnell and others smug in their evil,
as we feast on corrupt laws like ravenous weevils.
The anguish, the guilt, the tears and the sears;
no payment or healing all remains in arrears.
The little ones,
the tiny one's marching headlong,
a Mozart a baker a candlestick maker.
We dare not stare as they pass us by
their feeble cries reaching the skies.
Again, we fell for the original lie,
"eat of this you certainly won't die,"

our sacrifice of shame now numbs our soul pain.
God Himself must sort out this mess,
murder row lane and our legacy of shame.
These tiny martyrs He hides at the alter
singing a song and a lullaby psalter.
Lord please have mercy on me,
my unborn child now let me see,
it's all so confusing don't you agree?
I am sorry and repent,
it's Jesus you sent as He paid the ghastly cost,
so my soul is not lost.
My child is waiting for me to see.

Not Yet!

We almost lost the patriarch,
the grand old man was
rubbing elbows with the
angles. I was frightened, could
I carry his cloak?
Sitting at his bedside he
looked so frail and old- I
remembered him much younger;
hammering nails and doing
things with hands that now
are almost lifeless. But he has
an iron spirit and erstwhile
red hair. The wind comes with its song telling about
things given to be taken
away and given in another
form.
The vision breaks and the
child suddenly grows old he
is so close the bright
light beckons, he has been
here before.
he is most elegant in
his sunset. Kisses upon
the lips tears down the cheeks. Dying is such
tedious business- let's
forgo it for today.
Let's hug and kiss and
reminisce- see he's getting
stronger.

Grace and Wrath

It is a dreadful thing to fall into the hands of an angry God
as Edwards spoke in a sermon with an approving nod.
God is not good to all men,
but His will is to be good to some in the end.
He selects His elect it is true this being His sovereign rule.
Some men He made for the day of evil,
some he hated still in the womb so feeble.
His brother Jude instructs before of old,
some were ordained to condemnation we are told.
Others fitted to destruction as Peter instructs,
and appointed to wrath Paul also speaks about that.
Some like Judas go to their own place
as the Book of Acts plainly states.
Love and Justice, grace and wrath,
attributes of God that will forever last.

The Same Different as Me

Why do you hate me just as I am?
Is it you warp and weave or just your whim?
To hate you must know me well
with your assumptions and biases'
you send me to hell. Please take some time
to figure me out, I am not what you conjure, and I am not a lout.
I am sure I am similar to all of you,
with hopes, dreams and family it's true.
All men are capable of some evil,
our skin tones and colors don't make us so regal.
Take some time to get to know me,
and I'll do the same the next time you I see.

Martyred Saints

I am on the precipice of discontent;
which way to go?
I know my natural bent.
If I leap to this familiar place,
a place I know so well;
my smoldering rage now contained in its cage,
my soul being scarred and will not be assuaged.
But my reasons today are manifold,
as the martyred saints their stories are told.
I know well what your Scriptures say Lord,
that justice and revenge are all yours,
but my sinful flesh want's an eye for an eye,
as I struggle to realize it was your will they should die.
Your wisdom and knowledge are immeasurably vast
as I cling to my most familiar past.
This is one more time I must kneel and repent
of this my lingering discontent.
The battle just out of our sight;
Satan disguised like an angel of light,
his demons with their false righteousness,
as preachers,
teachers,
and seminarians too,
boldly teach against your holy rules;
as they lead men to go astray,
on Satan's wide road to his grandest of plays.
The saint's cry out from beneath your throne,
"how long Lord for our revenge",
we plead with them maranatha Lord,
our souls being scorched and very singed.

Little Boy and Daddy

Oh, my daddy long leagues apart,
the river Jordan had severed our hearts.
No more shall we speak of things shallow or deep, oh how I long
for one more time to meet.
I have questions to ask of you;
as a boy what did you do?
Motherless and fatherless you
were made of different stuff;
as a wandering little boy this would have been tough.
Riding box cars on the rails,
in the morning cold did you wail?
It's cold without a coat,
I am sure you missed your mother most.
Homeless in the depths,
did you have little boy dreams like the rest?
Any little friends you could share your dreams with,
or did you just keep them close to your breast?
Question daddy dear;
did you have a lot of fear;
you know you were always my dear.
As I ponder these things in my heart,
it's plain to see,
you're a hero to me.
As a vagabond, roamer and free
somehow you fathered and raised us three.
You did not cut, turn, and run,
when in truth things were not so very much fun.
Faithful in marriage and your work,

there is so much to learn from this old book.
Unlearned and rough around the edges
with no letters behind your name,
but to us it was plain even without fame,
we were proud to carry your name.
His friends often called him Red,
his roots from Eire, his twinkling eyes with hues of blue
an Irishman through and through.
Someday we shall meet again, and my questions will begin.
Daddy can you hark back to times long past?
This time I promise I will sit still
as you regale me with thrill after thrill.

A Fairy Tale

Lying upon my bed, settling down to dream;
I thought I heard a little scream,
But was it in my head?
There is something about this windy moor that takes away my breath,
Should I be worried about you, death?
As the cold wind claws and strokes this home,
I believe it would be a poor night to roam.
It's a night that fairies are about, and the banshee starts to keen;
stay away from my window you fairy queen,
you will not be catching my children's dreams.
My children sleeping upon their beds,
and in your hand they will not be led.
To your fairy lands beneath the moldering leaves,
the toadstools tall and the mosses and reeds,
where the fairies stand,
taking the children by their little hands.
Let's visit the trout and the salmon deep,
there we will find a quiet place to sleep.
Oh, dear child of Eire,
Awake and come to me.
Cut the web, it's just a thread and find your way home to me.
As the North Sea froths and the wind blows cold,
It's times like these that I feel old.
I remember the times when my ancestors believed,
The Emerald Isle rose from the sea.
Let me rest awhile my wife and me,
and warm our bones by these lovely old stones.

The wee ones rescued from fairy dreams as they found their way home
to me.
Be gone from my door with your sickle in hand,
This is where we will take our stand.
Your ghoulish face has not a trace of mirth or dancing jigs.
Be gone with you, I have much to do.
The sun is now coming fast,
the vapors rise from the dewy grass,
as the now becomes the past.
We have fended off another night with all its attended frights;
Leprechaun's banshee's and fairies too,
We bid you all a fair adieu.

Bible Story Part One

In the beginning God creates;
He made man not early but late.
Putting us in a perfect garden,
there was just one rule not up for bargain.
Our mother and father made a mistake it appears,
that's lasted eons and many a year.
They sinned and rebelled,
so, with God they could not dwell.
The first result of this terrible thing is
Abel was murdered by his brother Cain.
Man was to labor covered in shame,
as women were to bear children with labor and pain.
Adams manifesto was dominion you see,
and the earth was filled by his linage and seed.
Man's wickedness built like Babel on stilts,
his arrogance and sin reaching full hilt.
God confounded these people with various tongues,
as they pursued evil like beetles on dung.
Evil reached to the heavens so high
then God chose Noah to take a boat ride.
Noah preached about one hundred years,
but there was no repentance not even one tear.
God chose all things that would survive,
Noah and sons and four of their wives.
After the deluge the earth was cleansed,
all were dead there was little of sin;
but alas this would not last.
The second dove was sent out and did not return,

dry land was confirmed this Noah did learn.
It did not take long for these eight to repopulate.
Noah imbibed as Ham looked on,
it wasn't too long before all innocence was gone.
God looked on this problem of sin,
and knew this would be man's terrible end.
But He had His plan,
He chose Abram this pagan from a distant land.
He told Abram and Sari his wife that they would have offspring
like the stars of the night.
Now Abraham and now Sarah renamed by God
were dry and old and were prone to nod;
knowing there were no peas in the pod.
With Melchizedek, Lot, Gomorrah and Sodom,
our dear Abraham had reached his very bottom.
But after some laughter who did appear,
Isaac the son most highly one dear.
God said this is good now take him and slay;
let's just see how much you will pray.
Abraham God bless him was obedient to his Lord,
because Isaac was saved,
Israel was made.
God made a covenant with this most lovely man,
now Jews and Gentiles are included in his plan.
But the Israelites did not follow the Patriarchs of old,
sin entered in as this story unfolds.
Their disobedience cast them as slaves in exile,
four hundred years in Egypt is a very long while.
Moses this stuttering prince, a Jew in disguise,
had issues of anger now a quarreling man died.
Moses then fled to a faraway place,

but God said your eighty now let's turn back your face.
You will lead my people from Pharaoh's slave school;
you are now no longer a violent young fool.
Because of the plagues and miracles many,
God said I will lead you to a land of plenty.
As the Red Sea parted,
they ran and they darted.
Now on dry ground,
they heard Pharaoh's and army swallowed up by a sound.
God said look this Canaan is milk and honey,
but the spies could see only giants,
and they had the money.
But Joshua and Caleb said we can do this,
as they started to clean the land of the pagan misfits.
God was not pleased at Israel's lack of faith,
so, for forty years they wandered lost in this place.
Yahweh said these people need some rules
as He took old Moses to a mountainous school.
This was a most scary time,
no animals nor man were permitted to climb.
Moses was gone for a very long while
and when he came down the people were wild.
Even priestly Aaron who did make a calf,
the people had all become somewhat daft.
With the cloud by day and fire at night,
add ten laws all things will be right.
Since old Moses now dead, Joshua led;
filling the land with evil pagan dead.
The mandate that the Lord so required,
Israel failed to keep in its lustful desires.
When Joshua passed all the people gasped;

we will just do what we've done in the past.
As many people suffered and died,
God in his mercy and graciousness replied;
I've got covenants to keep but I know you all just cheat;
now Judges shall rule over you.
This went on for a long while then the people got tired;
they said Samuel "we want a king that's our desire".
God's lovely Samuel now this he could handle
but the people chose tall dark handsome Saul.
Now Saul was erratic and a bit peripatetic,
he conquered and slew and the Lord he eschewed.
Things became chaotic
and he was neurotic obsessed with sweet David boy.
But God told Samuel this meek shepherd is mine,
and the redeemer will come from his blood line.
This righteous king was mighty and bold;
Israel was nearing and close to its goal.
Bathsheba arrived then a long slide;
David left with pain and very much shame.
Dissension in his tent caused such a rent
now Israel was torn into two.
The kings of the North so evil and course,
the Prophets could not turn this tide;
these kings all drunk on their pride.
The Assyrians so cruel now Israel they ruled,
the good kings of Judah looked on.
But the Jews practiced evil which made them more feeble.
This rebellious people with whom God wanted to dwell,
to the Babylonians they eventually fell.
Daniel and friends stood fast to the last,
Nehemiah said let's rebuild the old walls.

They built walls and a Temple this now seemed so simple,
but God was not dwelling but gone.
The glory was not as with Isaiah of old,
nor clouds nor fire at night;
still in exile such a terrible fright.
For four hundred years not one word from the Lord"
Lord have you forgotten about us"?
But as the Prophet once said
"here comes one for the dead",
tatterdemalion John the baptizer man;
born of woman,
God said none was so grand.
He said here is Jesus the Lamb who removes sins from the damned.
The Dove testifies of His love from above.
The next thirty three years will be wild
and unique as He teaches, and for us He reaches.
But since we are mean we concoct such a scheme
only devils and demons could cheer.
Let's hang this man on a tree he means nothing to me.
The first half of the story ends here.
Let me catch my breath before I recite the rest;
act two will be a big test.

Healing

My son with rosy cheeks
his health slowly returning
leaping in the air watching
him play, boy's
games, kid's games- real
things.
I meter the time when he
will be sound of body and mind.
We almost lost him- he was
moving too fast, the child
overcome by serious things,
bigger than grown up child
robbing; the evils
snickering at us all.
My fists beating the air
sobbing, fighting for my son.
Let go and dance in the
warm air, cry softly and
nudge against me-l am
still here.

Baptism

Today's the day I publically display my allegiance to Jesus,
the Truth and the Way.
Standing at the entrance to the baptismal pool,
renouncing Satan and his evil rule.
Now robed in black I turn my back on Satan's ravenous feast,
and now face the saints,
both the great and the least.
I remove the dark robe and naked I stand,
entering the waters as a new man.
Buried with water and cleansed from my sin,
I arise with Jesus wanting much more of Him.
The Saint's greet me with cheers and tears,
and robe me in white to my joyous delight.

Confusion?

Life feels like a merry-go-round
as the righteous are often thrown to the ground;
the false- righteous uttering nary a sound.
Easy teaching abounds and tickles our ears;
hard sayings nowhere to be found.
Scriptures clear no muddling in there,
open your ears to hear.
There are only two sexes no matching nor mixes;
boy marries girl and they procreate,
that's how God in His wisdom creates.
You applaud you little demigods,
but prophets and apostles laid down the rules;
the truths from God's heavenly school.
The truth is the truth your feelings here take no root
as you plod on the path of the world.
Its wisdom is foolishness,
its philosophies are mute,
death always wins no time to be cute.
God is not mocked,
His word is the rock.
I must not despair as my thoughts race through the air;
it's Jesus I need the one who does care.

Friends

A mighty mountain rising from a plain,
is a person a moniker friend for a name.
Some linger a lengthy bit,
others gone in a hop and a skip,
but each serves a special need, a stanchion a pillar a wavering reed.
This one I would die for but now can get lost,
my needs are so fickle and comes at great cost.
I am fair weathered and so are they;
many file through but few will stay.
You must know me inside and out,
my shine and my stain my sin and my pout.
If you don't turn and depart from me,
if you don't faint from all that you see.
then I might gaze and discern upon you,
and judge you harshly to see what you do.
If you are still standing with love in your heart,
a friendship beginning a glorious start.
You seem to know me all pretense being gone;
I am just myself for this I have longed.
Know and being known no averting of eye,
you love me with all my warts and my sty.
This happens rarely a few times in one's life,
all others are fillers where drama is rife.
This one I know and they me,
speaking or silence whatever we please;
near or distant matters little to us,
boundaries and spatials are just a mere fuss.
Time goes by and the relationship grows,

our souls reverberating,
resonating love shows.
This good gift of God a foretaste of glory,
no shielding or veil just my blemished story.
I am as you see me needy and weak,
these saints these friends,
the one's that I seek.

A Name

Weaver of words please smith a name for me.
The name above every name;
its easy it's Jesus it is the best all other names simply laid to rest.
O Lord our Lord,
how majestic is your name in all the earth.
Your splendor your works not a scintilla of dearth.
Alpha, Omega, end of debate.
Standing before Him;
did you love Him or hate.

Friend and Guide

Let us view this in majestic skies that every mind with love doth rise.
The bright moon has seen and starlight with its sight,
have witnessed my prayers ascending at night;
a kind of tune that causes all fears to sway and swoon.
In the midst of tribulations and trials my failures I see as my feeble self-reels.
Come stand with me as you have never lost a battle in your holy array,
come lovely Jesus stand with me and stay.
We all have such sorrows to bear;
the Saints come beside us and these they will share.
Praising blessed Christ with my voice,
to him it's my wonderful choice.
I was wandering in sin when Jesus came in,
out went my shame as He called me by name,
and I shall never be the same.
When night draws near and long shadows appears,
my wont is always to fear,
but I see my savior drawing nigh and he is suddenly here.
He is my guide and my friend right to the very end.
Sans rapture this will be our test as the bands of death clutch at our breasts.
No more will we labor with rising breath
as we are sized by this messenger of death,
God will lead us by his beautiful eye,
I am sure of this till the day I die,
then I am with the sacred throng,
singing an everlasting mighty song.

Janie

How do I love thee let me count the way's
this is how we must start the poets all say.
Once upon a time I met not a Princess but a Queen,
awakening me from a nightmare to a wonderful dream.
From a long time ago and from a faraway place,
I came alive and this queen I embraced.
When we first met on the path that God set,
I fell in Love with this girl I just met.
Oh, how she laughed with sparkling eyes as she made me complete,
completely alive.
Now I said to myself don't sabotage this,
Janie fulfills all things on my list.
Stunningly beautiful with eyes pale blue and hair cut stylish of a
different hue.
My, such zeal for life all around when in her presence it's hard to be
down.
A short six-month courtship and then we were wed and off to Italy,
the place where we fled.
Now I see the world refreshed again,
looking through her glasses and rose-colored lens.
I am literally breathless being away all day.
And when I arrive home, we have so much to say.
Time is relentless on its journey through space,
just a few times when Grace touches our face.
An instance of this was on bended knee,
asking Janie dear would you marry me.
No more dragons to slay or castles to build,
but for my girl I would die on this hill.

We are so deeply and perfectly in love,
this has to be God's plan from far far above.
We don't need to have our way or always be right,
counting on one hand the times that we fight.
I am so comfortable and at peace with her,
seldom my soul is provoked to stir.
We are so alike this we have debated;
the possibility exists we might be related.
Up's and downs two cords tightly wound,
to the end we are bound and very sound.
We believed we were never going to grow old,
but age caught up and caused us to slow.
Age has made us go deeper still,
as thrills are stilled but our souls are filled.
I just really enjoy being around this girl,
our Ying and our Yang yes, it's the real thing.
God has given us twenty-one summers, winters and springs,
but it's in autumn I dream.
I won't try to describe the deep love I have for her,
words will fail,
of this I am sure.
She is so easy to be around, misplacing,
forgetting and seldom she frowns.
Banging and clanging going about her day;
I am resigned that is just her way.
She takes herself not seriously one bit,
laughing at herself just makes her a hit.
Friends dearly love her as she is slow to judge,
tending her garden without any drudge.
Innocent and beneficent these stories are told;
attributes of Janie that never grow old.

Wonderment surrounds her the world she lives in,
since I have known her that's the way it has been.
Richard, she says, place my bed outside,
to view God's creation as I take my last ride.
God, if you should take her first,
take me quickly for of her I would thirst.
As we both say our final farewell and goodbye's,
the birds she so loves sings us a sweet lullaby.
Oh God you know of her my love,
as we enter eternity with your most gentle shove.

Breath of Life

God creating man from the dust of the ground,
man, unable to move or make nary a sound.
Into his nostrils God breathed the mystery of His life,
now animated, man rose with wonder and delight.
The Breath that covered the waters,
now covered this man,
enabling him to walk,
run and to stand.
Like the Breath from the four winds,
breathed on those who were slain,
the dry bones in Ezekiel their life now regained.
Are we not just one breath away from death and our rest?
Love Him or hate Him will be your ultimate test.
In whose hand is the life of all living things,
is it not our Sovereign Lord,
who rules and ever reigns?
Christ Jesus breathing out His life on the cross,
the Father so demanded this would be the cost.
In the tomb for three days,
no breath in his lungs,
all sin laid on Him as He was strung out and hung.
Three days later,
the Spirit breathed Life back into this man,
now rising from the tomb with Jesus we can stand.
This Second Adam breathing life into those who believe,
sin and death fall away to our joy and great relief.
As the Psalms teach us,
let everything praise the Lord.
This being my great pleasure now and forevermore.

My Church

My church my splendid redoubt,
the place I worship and cast out my doubts.
The church being a hospital for all of us sinners,
struggling, overcoming trying to be winners.
The glory of the Gospel being just this,
all broken people come here to be fixed.
Preaching the Gospel of the Glorious Christ,
singing songs of praise three times or twice.
Fencing the table and baptized aright,
causes Satan and demons to leave and take flight.
The saints checking their pride at the door,
come seeking the balm that heals their poor souls.
Desperate for Jesus and a sermon that cut's,
everything I need to escape the worlds rut.
My friends are here doing the same as me,
restructuring our lives upon our knees.
I love my pastor and the elders too,
as they guide us in this heavenly school.
The Gospel, Sacraments and discipline here,
the marks of a true church of which we adhere.
Hard truths, God's truth spoken in Love,
offering salvation from the Spirit above.
God's church thriving always eternal,
standing athwart of all that's infernal.
Praising my most holy King,
in my church with saint's,
our anthem does ring.

The Evil in Me

When I see man contending with man,
It occurs to me; we must have a plan.
As I harrumph most sanctimoniously,
The truth of the matter the problem is me.
Evil has found a most receptive home,
both in my heart and inside my dome.
It is always lurking just inside,
I will feed it my flesh till the day I die.
I will judge this or that with my prideful eyes,
my poor fellow man has nowhere to hide.
I wield the sword of judgement so fine,
one would believe I am almost divine.
But God ask a question as he did of Job,
and in an instance my heart was disrobed.
Man is made in the Imago Dei,
but truth be known, we have nothing to say.
Without Jesus and his healing hands,
I would die in this sin and it would be my end.
My heart is devious above all things,
as I struggle to stay in the narrow lane.
My foot starts to slip, I am about to fall,
but Jesus by my side is standing so tall.
This remnant of sin will remain in me,
till' I cross over into eternity.

Luke

Oh, Luke from the very start,
you went and captured my heart,
from your earliest mewling and softest cry,
for you I know I would surely die.
From your arrival upon the scene
I knew that this would certainly mean a change in course for sure,
as you cast a most powerful lure.
You were a joy to be around with your laughter and little boy frown.
Playing hide and go seek with family and me hiding
with bottom up in the air,
being found again and again,
you said this doesn't seem fair.
As a toddler you ran with a most peculiar gate;
arms pumping up and down,
but you did run straight;
eyes set in flint you will surely finish this sprint.
Smells you held so dear and fast,
it seems mine was one that would last.
We bonded very fast and tight,
to this day it's all to my great delight.
A boy that's very humble and bright;
I want all the world to see what this boy means to me.
Luke being sober and quite through and through,
but oh, the love he has inside for me and for you.
He playing football with his buddies by his side,
victory upon victory;
I am not one to lie.
Possibilities for you to do abound as you stand about an around.

66

Being a child of God as you grow,
he will take you by the hand and show you the path to go.
A protector of your sisters
that's where you take a stand and those who lack a helper
you take them by the hand.
God is growing you into a very special man.

Time

A day worth living. Tomorrow
matching or excelling today, yesterday
remaining a reflection of now
so why confuse?
Why must we confuse today with yesterday
or tomorrow?
Tomorrow mustering abreast with hope,
mindful of losing the eonic race- jangling,
jumbling, jousting headlong into eternity.
Today surviving only narrowly, a shaft
separating tomorrow from yesterday, a fiber
burdening itself with the sinews of
mankinds misery and joy. A low struggle
and today melts into yesterday.
Yesterday aimlessly wandering, only to
be imperiled by a wandering mind, to be
gleaned of all that was today

Communism

Communism, a phantasmagoria of mans fevered imaginations;
the misery and defeat of man and many nations.
Marx's truculent notion a deadly swill and potion,
fed to the gormless masses as if eating honey and molasses.
Whittaker Chambers knowing firsthand the dangers of this belief,
spent the remainder of his life a relief he sought and beseeched.
Hundreds of millions of people enslaved,
automons marching mindlessly to their graves.
Nothing redeemable about this evil system,
the people being led refusing to listen.
God being the antithesis of all of this,
but Satan's scheme a hit not a miss.
When man in Gods image inverted his plan,
he moulded his god in the image of man.
Their empty eidolon I freely grant them,
but their nescience striving just leads to their end.
Lenin gloating socialism is communism lite,
we the free must muster to fight,
what God ordained is just and just right.
Pol Pot, Stalin and Mao too,
the leftist professors in all of our schools;
Chavez, Madura, Castro also,
all of Satan's minions take them in tow,
throw them all out and let people go.
This perverse philosophy scorching the earth,
but God's beauty blends with mirth,
adding goodness to things of earth.
Peace comes dropping very slow,
in God's presence his heavenly glow.

Unknowable God

A distant nebula exploding in space,
a miniscule atom oscillating in place.
A cold dead stone,
the sea rife with life.
All that we see fills with delight.
We try to discern as we go deeper
but unraveling these mysteries makes us just weaker.
We puff and assume we will figure this out
when in fact our stirrings all come to naught.
Since we ourselves are created beings,
the answers to these mysteries will never be seen.
Philosophies, science, man's imaginations too,
all propelled and powered by pride this is true.
There is only one God and we are not He,
we know nothing at all can't we agree?
We should submit under His sovereign eye,
building towers of praise towards His azure skies.

Spring

The chimes are charming tinkling and clanging,
deepening to a resonating richness each trying to be heard;
a symphony of freshness. Oh, I like the deep tones the best,
but I do confess I like all the rest.
The wind flutters and dies, as it drives the music correctly on time,
chime after charming chime.
The wind hastens from where?
But then it's quickly gone from here.
Whence to thence?
The old trees nod an approving yes all dressed in their very best;
The maples and Nandina's all dressed in their reds,
the Photina's say "don't forget about us",
we're not much of a fuss.
The Abelia's say" well-we have three colors to display",
while the Mahonia pleads "look at my leaves and please don't delay."
The thrift with its bright pink gives all a quick wink.
The proud apple and cherry trees in splendid array,
"we are all so beautiful won't you just say?"
The peonies are poking their cute little heads,
up from the soil with effortless toil;
it appears they have done this before.
Tiger Lily's and butterflies abound,
a mallard and hen just floating around.
The sun is warming me gently with heat as all creation is in rhythm
and beat.
The majestic blue spruce is stately and demure,
as oaks tower over all with a statement for sure.
Such anticipation is in the air, as every living thing with a nudge,

and a dare leaps forth without so much as a care.
The greens are outstanding variations untold,
whoever thought this up was ever so bold.
Olive to emerald the faintest of greens,
mixing the golds and the reds in between.
Now let me think what could set off this sight;
a bird, and a wasp, and a bee makes it right.
A grey tufted titmouse a sparrow white crowned;
a red bellied woodpecker just hanging around.
The cardinal is skittish, the finch speaks just Yiddish,
the blue bird stand-offish the jay is just bossy.
The dove with its mournful coo;
these birds have plenty to do.
The vultures above,
the raptor chasing the dove its nonstop action we see.
All this with a seamless and perfect fit.
The scene comes together by each wonderful bit.
The sun starts to set, and my soul is at rest,
this star turns the tree tops a gold.
First you must start to slow down your heart and listen and see anew,
as all of this comes into view.
Et tu? Me too. Yes! You too.
I sense God is the master of this as I lie down in wonderful bliss.

What is Life?

What is Life but a collection of endeavors,
disappointments and sometimes laughter.
Weaving strains of sadness and bleak reality
of depression.
Must we sit? Ineptly sentenced by our past,
waiting, grasping, frustrated.
Life is too brief, not to live it richly must
be immoral. But failures and beginnings
are realities; to be immuned from these
honors is to die prematurely. To struggle
above these agonies is to behold Life in its
fullest- a Janus appearance of reality
and idealism.
Compromise must be moderate. If the mood
is present, be sad but rejoice with me.
Push, push back at the Gorgons of Life, but
have in attendance the Graces. Laugh, laugh
loudest with me.
Record in your mind the shortcomings of Life,
excuse mine. Be unafraid, reach out for
Love, it is the first virtue
Find room for me.

Redeemed

This path I have trod so far away from my God.
I repent with bitter tears the many wasted precious years.
My sin and straying,
Lord, my heart is sick and sore.
My only hope my only plea is my Jesus died for me.
As Jesus passes by this way,
my stubborn heart still delays;
I will wait just another day.
I know his voice is so true,
I know my heart will still refuse.
Jesus it seems it's up to you,
there is not much that I can do.
You chose and then you died for us your only lovely bride;
in your sheltered wings we run to hide.
My heart bursts forth when I consider this,
all joy, mercy and beauty is on this heavenly list.
I will be face-to-face without shielding or veil,
my Savior and me this He said will not fail.
Your promises are a part of you,
your heart is always so true.
Send me forth to worlds unknown,
where your beauty and might will be shown.

Love

The seasons change, and things
occur, time stops and starts, errily
cadenced with my heart, tenuous
and sensuous.
Now, being a narrow shaft
separating yesterday from tomorrow
this time I live requires love
to keep me rooted in the now.
Strange, but when all things
are distilled to the basic essence,
it is love. Love so simple but
immeasurably profound, the true
joy of man, it makes me soar
it makes me give, it makes me
want to live- nothing more
Remembering that love is patient
and love is kind, I know
that I will always love.

Leaving

As I lay my head on this pillow of death,
and I lie down to my final rest;
no philosophies or teachings will suffice
the master of death is never so nice.
My whole person is in abject despair;
he will grab and pull it doesn't seem fair.
This Prince of Demons has won this war,
as I prepare to finally pass through the door.
I am frightened and seem all alone,
but into my room my Lord has flown.
My wife, my children, my friends and me,
we really have nothing to offer to thee.
Right now, my soul is laid so bare,
there is nothing about me that seems so fair.
I do not want to row over the river Styx,
my arms are as strong as withered old sticks.
But you reach out with your human hand,
all of this and more you understand.
You lift me up with the holes in your hands,
as I hear the strains of angelic bands.
I feel the death grip and chains fall away,
at this moment there is nothing much left to pray.
Into Behula land I fly with Gods tender delight,
Jesus my lord I never imagined this sight.
God says welcome most highly esteemed,
come and sit in remembrance of me.
The times that you spoke or thought upon me,
it's all written down so all can see.

The times you opened a door,
or hitched your plow and pulled with the poor.
When you wept with the one behind bars;
imagined or real they are what they are.
Every mummering prayer that drifted up to us,
it was like holy scented heavenly dust.
There are saints here you have never met,
but because of you many we still get.
So much in this book to reveal,
it will take eternity to read as you kneel.
But up for now you have work to do,
unknown worlds beckons to you.
Siblings, children, and parents will view,
all things in heaven have been renewed.

www.ingramcontent.com/pod-product-compliance
Lightning Source LLC
Chambersburg PA
CBHW050429290526
45786CB00003B/1452